*STRATEGIC PLANNING FOR
COLLEGES AND UNIVERSITIES:
A Systems Approach
to Planning
and Resource Allocation*

STRATEGIC PLANNING FOR COLLEGES AND UNIVERSITIES:
A Systems Approach to Planning and Resource Allocation

John C. Merson

Robert L. Qualls

TRINITY UNIVERSITY PRESS • SAN ANTONIO

The Trinity University Press gratefully acknowledges the assistance of the Winthrop Rockefeller Foundation in making this book possible.

To
Carolyn and Lorraine

FOREWORD

Many colleges and universities are in financial trouble. While the problems faced by independent institutions with small endowments are more visible, state-supported institutions will also experience severe fiscal pressures as the size of the college-bound pool declines and as state legislatures respond to growing resistance from taxpayers.

Colleges and universities that are weak financially are likely to be the first to close. By wisely utilizing available resources and tailoring services to new and broader constituencies, some institutions may be able to substitute imagination and competence for money and to eliminate fiscal strength as the primary determinant of survival.

The goals of the Winthrop Rockefeller Foundation are reflected in its support of this publication. Progress in building more effective institutions, broadening participation in decision-making, and promoting economic and community development depends on sound organizational planning, including the definition of mission and purposes, selection of specific objectives, design of programs and administrative procedures, and the evaluation of service delivery and quality.

The approach proposed in this book offers governing boards and top administrators an action-oriented tool for systematically asking the right questions about what they are doing, why, and how well it is being done. When institutions make a serious commitment to answering these questions, they are more likely to innovate in the way they serve the public welfare. They are also better able to justify their claims for public and philanthropic support.

While the system described here is designed specifically for colleges and universities, its general thrust is equally applicable to governmental and private nonprofit agencies in other areas in which the Foundation has an interest: rural development, community education and organization, housing rehabilitation, environmental protection, and equalization of employment opportunities. In every area where organizations are established and funded to serve the public interest, a systematic approach to management is needed to ensure a continuing process of adaptation to changes in the organization's external environment, renewal or redefinition of purposes, and development of innovative programs.

Thomas C. McRae, President
Winthrop Rockefeller Foundation
Little Rock, Arkansas
January, 1979

CONTENTS

LIST OF EXHIBITS

PREFACE

The critical issue facing colleges and universities is how to reallocate resources in accordance with demographic and economic trends and developments that are changing the market for higher education. Each institution must accomplish this task, whether it seeks to maintain its existing role or to carve out a new niche in the increasingly competitive market for higher education. Planning procedures currently in use are not well suited to resolve the urgent questions of programming and market positioning. As a result, many colleges are experiencing crises that affect both their educational effectiveness and their financial health.

This book describes a set of techniques that colleges and universities can use in analyzing the educational environment in which they operate, deciding which segments of it to serve and how to do so, and monitoring their effectiveness in pursuing established objectives. Taken as a whole, these techniques comprise a system of planning and resource allocation procedures that link together the key tasks of managing an institution of higher education.

The techniques presented in this book are designed for use by academic administrators and members of governing boards of colleges and universities. These are the individuals responsible for leading their institutions in developing and implementing plans required to resolve critical strategic and organizational issues.

With the support of the Winthrop Rockefeller Foundation, the authors developed the system described here to provide management tools that would help institutions of higher education identify public needs more effectively. The project benefited from the responses and comments of presidents from thirty-five colleges and universities in Arkansas and eleven surrounding states. These administrators participated in a seminar and workshop session at which the system was first presented. Others who contributed insights and made valuable suggestions included William H. Bell, an attorney and a trustee of Trinity University in San Antonio, Texas, and the University of Tulsa in Tulsa, Oklahoma; William A. Shoemaker, vice-president of The Council for the Advancement of Small Colleges; and Joseph C. Inman, a vice-president of the management consulting firm of Merson Associates, Inc.

In developing the concepts and procedures proposed here, the authors drew heavily on their experience in managing and providing management counsel to a wide variety of public and independent colleges and universities. Additionally, they examined planning practices which have proven useful in noneducational settings. A planning system developed by one of the authors has been used extensively and with good results by both banks and educational institutions. Colleges and financial institutions share a number of significant characteristics: both provide services as opposed to producing tangible products; both are regulated and strongly influenced by governmental policies and procedures; both are affected by location and geographic surroundings; finally, both are experiencing dynamic changes which threaten the survival of individual organizations. The authors also adapted a number of aspects of business planning systems, including those which have been implemented in large, diversified, and decentralized corporations. In such settings, planning has been fully integrated with other management tasks and has been institutionalized as a regular process linked both to budgeting and to managerial control.

The presentation of the material begins with a description of key aspects of the external educational, economic, and social environment to which colleges and universities must adapt their programs and services. Chapter 1 also discusses the weaknesses of existing planning practices and indicates why a new approach is needed.

Chapter 2 presents an overview of the proposed planning and resource allocation system and describes the four stages of the cycle. It also suggests benefits which could result from the system's implementation.

Chapters 3 and 4 discuss the planning and resource allocation process in more detail, first considering the approach and methods of analysis and decision-making and then focusing on the assignment of tasks to specific parts of the organizational structure. Particular attention is given in Chapter 3 to the role of the governing board, since the trend toward a more active role for board members is increasingly evident in the areas of policy-making and planning for the institution's major programs and services.

Chapter 5 provides guidance in two areas: first, adapting the system for use by individual institutions, and second, integrating its operations with other administrative processes.

John C. Merson
Robert L. Qualls
January, 1979

STRATEGIC PLANNING FOR COLLEGES AND UNIVERSITIES:
A Systems Approach to Planning and Resource Allocation

BACKGROUND 1

Both the nature and the level of demand for higher education are changing. These changes are partly demographic and partly a reflection of the attitudes of new participants in postsecondary learning. Other changes are occurring in the areas of institutional governance; the sources and amounts of financial assistance to dependent and independent students; staff relations and collective bargaining; consumer purchasing habits; voluntary support of institutions by alumni, foundations, and businesses; the availability of professional managers who can administer educational programs. These changes are exerting an impact on all areas of institutional operations, and one result is that planning practices traditionally employed are no longer functioning optimally.

This chapter provides a perspective for the balance of the book by describing key aspects of the environment in which colleges and universities are operating. Further, it analyzes several areas in which planning practices currently in use fail to help institutions adapt to changes in their environment.

THE CHANGING ENVIRONMENT OF HIGHER EDUCATION

The environment within which colleges and universities operate has been undergoing a series of interrelated changes in seven areas:

- Market Demand
- Governance
- Student Financial Aid
- Consumer Behavior
- Staff Relations and Collective Bargaining
- Charitable Giving
- Management Talent

Market Demand

Following a period of unprecedented growth in the 1960s and early 1970s due to social and demographic factors, enrollment has stabilized in most institutions and has even declined in some. Reflecting a decrease in the number of births during the late 1950s, and also in the proportion of high school graduates seeking college admission, total enrollment in the nation's 3,000 colleges and universities is projected to begin declining in the early 1980s. For an individual campus, a drop in enrollment of as little as 5 percent could be disastrous, given the high levels of fixed costs that are characteristic of higher education. More than 100 colleges closed or merged with other institutions between 1970 and 1978, even though total postsecondary enrollment was increasing during that period. Equally as important to colleges as trends in total enrollment are changes in the age mix, attendance status, and educational objectives of the student population. Increased proportions of older, part-time, and nondegree students will exercise a significant influence on the nature of demand for postsecondary education and on the types of programs and administrative support required to meet this demand.

Governance

The governance of higher education is changing in several respects. First, as many observers have noted, higher education is more heavily affected by state and federal taxes and regulations than was formerly the case. References to the tax-exempt status of colleges are misleading when one notes that they are subject, directly or indirectly, to a variety of sales, excise, and payroll taxes. In addition, regulations covering affirmative action in admissions and employment, retirement, age and sex discrimination, equal employment opportunity, the treatment of handicapped persons, and occupational health and safety all impose constraints on institutional decision-making which must be taken into account in the planning process.

Second, campuses that are part of statewide systems enroll a large and growing share of all students. State-level governing boards and commissions are enlarging their authority over institutional programs, services, and funding decisions in response to pressures from the executive and legislative branches of state governments. These same governing boards and commissions often are responsible for administering scholarship and loan programs serving students enrolled at independent colleges, as well as for approving new degree programs in all institutions. While these trends may appear to narrow the scope of decision-making by individual campus trustees and administrators, their primary effect in fact is to complicate such decisions and the analyses that must precede them. Because the number of external influences to be taken into account is increased, the lead time required for major decisions is lengthened, indicating the need for a more systematic planning process.

Finally, there are indications that state-level coordinating boards might begin requiring individual campuses to set forth their objectives and operating plans in explicit and perhaps even measurable terms, in response to growing pressures from taxpayers to cut spending in areas where accomplishments do not justify costs. Some state commissions are exploring ways to allocate funds to institutions at least partly on the basis of performance, rather than solely on the basis of enrollment and indirect costs.

Student Financial Aid

The revolution in student financial aid has been gaining momentum for nearly twenty years and is still not complete. The task of paying for higher education was once viewed as the primary responsibility of students and their families who received only limited help from private funds channeled through college admissions offices. Primary responsibility for meeting the tuition bill now has shifted to federal and state grant and loan programs. The increasing enrollment in institutions funded primarily by state and local taxes reflects and strengthens the widespread attitude that providing the opportunity for higher education is a governmental responsibility. The expansion of eligibility for federal student aid programs to cover students from middle-income families and the strong support for tuition tax credits indicate broad acceptance of the concept of public funding for students in all institutions and at all levels. Institutions therefore are under pressure to increase their tuition and other charges to ensure that the yield from external aid programs is maximized. With nearly half of all college students receiving some type of financial aid, and with much of this aid coming from government-sponsored aid programs, colleges and universities should anticipate the arrival of permanent federal guidelines covering maximum tuition levels allowable for computing aid awards. Some states have already established limits on increases in community college tuition and fee levels. Because student aid programs managed outside the individual college account for such a large share of college revenues, planners and decision-makers need to approach systematically the task of ensuring that future developments in these aid programs will not threaten institutional stability or effectiveness.

Consumer Behavior

The revolution in consumer behavior affecting marketers of other goods and services is also making its presence felt in higher education. From a marketing standpoint, college is a "big ticket" or major purchase made directly by the ultimate user. As is the case with other industries that are highly visible and subject to a myriad of state and federal regulations, colleges must be prepared to defend their promotional publications and other advertising, the size and frequency of their price increases, and their stated or implied claims for product effectiveness. This last, for example, will require institutions to be able to document the specific results of their operations and the benefits derived by students. To address these concerns, institutions must have in place procedures for specifying their objectives and measuring the actual outcomes of their academic programs, and for monitoring internally any changes in academic program performance that may have implications for customer relations.

Staff Relations and Collective Bargaining

As employee associations have increased their membership in recent years, and as collective bargaining has been established in

more states, the conduct of labor relations in higher education
has changed visibly and dramatically. Strikes and threats of
strikes have eroded much of the basis for collegial governance.
The trend toward union representation has coincided with long-
term improvement in the economic status of faculty members,
nonacademic employees, and administrators. Institutions have
lost some of their control over staff compensation levels, and this
cost category can no longer be treated as a discretionary item in
balancing budgets. Instead, compensation levels are negotiated
through collective bargaining or meet-and-confer procedures and
then fixed by contract. These procedures generally have the effect of making it more difficult for institutions to control the costs
of employee benefits or to increase productivity levels. There is
also a greater tendency for employees at one institution to seek
comparability in compensation with prevailing levels at other institutions in the same state or region, regardless of differences in
the economic circumstances of institutions. As a result, there
arises a greater need to consider environmental and comparative
trends in institution-wide planning and to tie program and financial plans to considerations of staffing, personnel costs, the
relative balance of unions and management, and employee
attitudes.

Charitable Giving

While changes in labor relations have been well-publicized,
developments in the field of charitable giving have been largely
masked by inflation. In real terms, adjusted for inflation's bite, individual giving to private nonprofit institutions and social-service
organizations is running at an annual rate of $8 billion less than it
was in 1960. While voluntary private support of higher education
still exceeds $2 billion annually, gifts for current operating pur-
poses have not kept pace with inflation. In fact, the level of annual support as a proportion of total operating revenues has been
declining for more than fifteen years. In order to cushion the effect of this loss, colleges have been committing a larger share of
their total voluntary support to operating needs. This practice
means that less is available to build an endowment for future
years. Consequently, although the problem of making up for lost
endowment earnings may be deferred for several years, it is not
solved. Endowment income, which is essentially income from
prior years' gifts, has dropped from 4 to 2 percent of colleges' current revenues over the last 25 years. In the absence of new
growth in charitable giving, which may not be forthcoming, col-

leges are facing major questions of financial strategy. They will come to rely more heavily on tuition and governmental appropriations. Such dependence on tuition implies that they will need to develop a strong marketing orientation, while growing reliance on public funds suggests that institutions will face greater difficulty in maintaining control over decisions on the nature and scope of programs and services. Whatever the outcome, there is clearly a need to anticipate and prepare for more complex contingencies.

Management Talent

The seventh and last of the revolutions affecting higher education is taking place in the area of management talent. As graduate schools of public and business administration have come to appreciate the distinctive aspects of management in the nonprofit sector, they have begun to help prepare large numbers of experienced professionals and middle-managers for senior administrative positions. As a result, colleges and universities will not need to rely as heavily in the future on scholars and teachers recruited for administrative posts late in their careers. At the same time, the growing availability of professional administrators should make it possible for institutions to adapt and implement more readily the techniques of modern management.

THE NEED FOR A NEW APPROACH TO PLANNING

By and large, planning procedures currently in use in colleges and universities do not give adequate attention to the environmental changes discussed above. First, many colleges lack formal planning systems which provide for the regular review of strategic decisions made in prior years. Second, most planning systems merely document the consensus already existing within the institution on what programs and services should be offered, to whom, and within what levels of cost. Even the more recently developed planning, programming, and budgeting systems for higher education have been used largely to answer the question of what it will cost in the future to continue offering existing programs and to launch certain new programs. While such forward planning for these activities helps the organization to understand the long-term implications of commitments already made or presently under consideration, it does not serve the purpose of ensuring that the organization is pursuing appropriate objectives or that it is following a sound strategic approach to achieving these objectives.

Traditionally, college and university planning efforts have focused too much on "doing things right" and too little on "doing the right things." More specifically, traditional planning methods exhibit six weaknesses which prevent colleges from achieving maximum effectiveness in serving demonstrated public needs:

- Excessively complex analytical and administrative requirements
- Internal focus, rather than a market orientation
- Lack of attention to improving communications and building commitment
- Infrequent review and revision, and hence too time-consuming and cumbersome at each occurrence.
- Absence of a clear link between planning and budgeting
- Failure to provide for regularly reporting and evaluating results obtained

The planning techniques tried by many colleges have been highly complex in their requirements for data-gathering, analysis, and documentation of program proposals. As a result, planning has frequently become a paper-intensive, impersonal, and highly technical process which runs the risk of collapsing under its own weight. The difficulty of administering the process and of reaching timely conclusions and decisions has often produced intense frustration among participants, as well as a tendency for line administrators to try to shift the burden of planning to staff assistants. This results in a separation between planning and decision-making and renders planning activity less useful to managers. It also makes planning a more expensive and demanding administrative function. Underlying this is the failure to focus planning on the few major strategic issues and questions facing the organization.

A second weakness exhibited by current approaches to planning is their internal focus. Internally oriented planning systems most often have current programs as the starting point and concentrate on projecting the costs and revenues associated with the continuation of these programs. Where revenue deficiencies are found, planners focus on identifying new sources of funds or on how to increase support from existing sources. As a result, little attention is given to determining how developments occurring in the organization's external environment are affecting the demand or need for current programs and services. The focus of planning therefore is misdirected; by concentrating on the future scale and funding of its programs, the organization fails to consider whether these are in fact the "right" programs, the ones which best serve its underlying mission and purposes.

A third weakness of the planning practices widely followed in educational institutions is that their style is primarily analytical; that is, emphasis on the contents of plans rather than on the organizational process through which groups of people build shared commitments to achieving specific objectives. Unless planning efforts facilitate such team-building, there is little likelihood that planned objectives will be met. Organizations tend to neglect this behavioral or human dimension of planning when planning is defined primarily as an analytical function, to be assigned to isolated staff groups, or when the focus of attention is on the end-product, the planning document, rather than on the process itself. Excessive emphasis on the analytical side of planning separates planning from other administrative tasks and speeds up the actual work of planning. However, by neglecting the human dimension, the planning system will not be integrated into the organization's structure of responsibilities and decision-making patterns. Essential group processes are overlooked, and team-building does not occur.

Fourth among the deficiencies of existing planning practices is the reliance on intensive yet infrequent attacks on major issues, rather than on a regular planning cycle which can be integrated with other management processes. Where an organization institutes planning efforts irregularly and infrequently, there is a tendency to attempt too much in one iteration of the process. This also leaves plans unquestioned and unchanged for long periods of time. Instead of accepting planning as a routine management function, organizations utilizing such an intensive planning process view it as an exhausting task. As a consequence, the burden of planning often shifts to specialized staff groups who only function fully during the peak periods of planning activity. A more serious effect of this infrequency is that most administrators and faculty leaders fail to develop either proficiency in planning or a commitment to implementing plans. It frequently takes two or three iterations of a regular planning cycle for most administrators to develop high levels of expertise in both the analytical and team-building dimensions of the process. Moreover, an irregular planning effort, unlike a regular planning cycle, lacks provision for review, updating, and revision of previously prepared plans, often by the same people responsible for their initial formulation.

The lack of direct linkage between planning and budgeting procedures demonstrates inadequacy in a fifth area. Since budgeting occurs on a regular annual schedule, and since planning is generally intermittent, workable arrangements rarely exist to ensure that long-range goals are translated into annual operating plans and made the basis of annual budgets. Conversely, there can be no assurance that annual budgets reflect strategic plans previously developed or that the activities approved in the budget will move the organization closer to attaining its goals and objectives.

A final weakness frequently observed in college and university planning systems is the absence of formal provision for reporting program outcomes to managers and governing boards, comparing these to planned targets, and evaluating the results in relation to resources expended. This means that planning all too often becomes a bureaucratic exercise in which the wisdom of the original program decisions goes unquestioned, and the performance of responsible administrators is not appraised in terms of the results obtained from a given pattern of resource allocation.

Individually and in combination, all of these deficiencies seriously limit the potential value of most existing planning practices.

OVERVIEW   2

The proposed planning and resource allocating cycle divides planning and resource allocation tasks into four separate but carefully linked stages that in turn yield four primary benefits: a more effective use of resources, a longer range perspective for decision-making, better identification of high priority programs, and development of capable administrators.

The four stages are: diagnosis, planning, resource allocation, and evaluation. Exhibit I illustrates schematically the sequence of work throughout the cycle. Under the direction of the institution's executive team, each stage produces concrete answers to particular questions that, once resolved, define the work to be done in the next stage. At the end of each stage a brief report summarizes work performed, findings and conclusions reached, and the recommended actions or decisions. This report is then transmitted by the institution's president to its board of trustees. Following review by the board, the trustees can either approve the report or return it to the president for further consideration.

This chapter emphasizes the general purposes and expected outcomes of each of the four stages. The specific tasks required at each stage will be described in detail in the next chapter.

Stage I - Diagnosis

The first stage of the cycle assesses the current health of the institution and identifies both actual and potential problem areas. The most important outcome of this stage should be a list of specific issues, dealing with enrollment, programs, and finances, to be resolved during the balance of the planning process. In effect, these issues become the institution's planning agenda, with each defined as a question requiring a concrete action or series of actions.

An additional result of this diagnostic stage should be that administrators and faculty members will become more aware of major trends and developments occurring in the external environment of the organization. The diagnosis also should clarify the relative position of the institution within the postsecondary education system as a whole.

To prepare adequately for the beginning of each planning cycle, the institution needs to construct a data base of information

Exhibit I

STAGES IN THE PLANNING AND

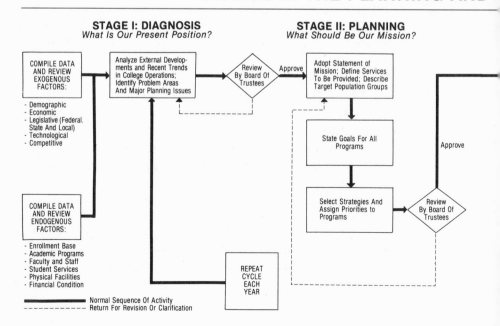

that, when shared among all participants in the process, will facilitate communication and agreement on problems and issues facing the institution. Exhibit II lists many of the items of information needed in a planning data base.

The end product of this stage is a brief report from the executive team to the board of trustees summarizing major trends in operations, principal external developments, and issues to be resolved during subsequent stages of the planning process.

Stage II - Planning

In the second stage of the cycle, the institution determines its mission, general goals, and strategic choices. This stage corresponds to the strategic planning steps carried out by well-managed industrial corporations and financial institutions.

The end product of this stage is a statement by the executive team that describes the institution's mission, goals, strategies, overall operating policies, and relative program priorities. When this statement has been approved by the board of trustees, it is broadly distributed within the institution and among its key external constituencies.

RESOURCE ALLOCATION CYCLE

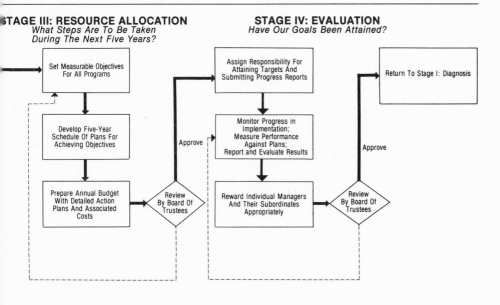

STAGE III: RESOURCE ALLOCATION
What Steps Are To Be Taken During The Next Five Years?

STAGE IV: EVALUATION
Have Our Goals Been Attained?

Set Measurable Objectives For All Programs

Develop Five-Year Schedule Of Plans For Achieving Objectives

Prepare Annual Budget With Detailed Action Plans And Associated Costs

Approve

Review By Board Of Trustees

Assign Responsibility For Attaining Targets And Submitting Progress Reports

Monitor Progress in Implementation; Measure Performance Against Plans; Report and Evaluate Results

Reward Individual Managers And Their Subordinates Appropriately

Approve

Review By Board Of Trustees

Return To Stage I: Diagnosis

ELEMENTS OF A MOD[

	EXOGENOUS FACTORS				
DEMOGRAPHIC	ECONOMIC	LEGISLATIVE	TECHNOLOGICAL	EDUCATIONAL	COMPETITIVE (A)
• Birthrates • Migration • Urbanization • Age distribu- tion • Population growth rates within service areas • Trends in sibling squeeze • Attitudes towards value and role of higher education	• Employment • Key industries • Demand for college graduates by field of study • Labor force characteris- tics • Earnings • Length of workweek • Annual changes in price indexes • Estimated family budgets	• Federal and state support for institutions, facilities, and student aid programs • Local support for communi- ty colleges • Federal, state and local aid to public schools • State planning and funding procedures	• Educational television • Computer networks • Media services • Use of tech- nology by se- condary schools, colleges, and universities • Education research and development • Transporta- tion systems	• High school completion rates • College attendance (participa- tion) rates by sector of post- secondary education • Level of educational attainment of adults, by age group • College Selection Factors	• Enrollment by institution and segment of post- secondary education • Tuition and other charges • Programs and curricular offerings • Location and service areas • Facilities • Faculty and management resources • Social and extra- curricular activities • Community resources • Competing Institutions

(A) Includes all institutions serving target student population.

NNING DATA BASE

ENDOGENOUS FACTORS					
ENROLLMENT	**ACADEMIC PROGRAMS**	**FACULTY AND STAFF**	**PHYSICAL FACILITIES**	**FINANCIAL PROFILE**	**STUDENT SERVICES**
• Student recruitment by source, level, and characteristics • Cost per applicant and matriculant • Enrollment by level • Enrollment by geographic, academic and socio-economic characteristics • Enrollment by resident and commuting status • Attrition by level, student characteristics, and program	• Degree programs offered by size, level and outcomes • Adult and continuing education programs • Cost per credit, student, and degree, by program • Special programs • Disposition and employment of graduates, by program • Instructional productivity, by program	• Faculty resources by program and division • Faculty compensation, rank, and tenure • Management, planning, investment and other staff resources • Age and sex distribution of faculty and staff	• Plant capacity (resident and commuting students) • Plant condition and operating costs, by faculty • Academic equipment, media, and other learning resources • Facilities and equipment for extracurricular activities • Unfunded depreciation • Annual depreciation	• Revenue and expense by function and program • Government support, by function • Voluntary support, by source, type, and size of gift • Auxiliary enterprises • Changes in fund balances • Tuition and other charges • Financial aid resources • Endowment	• Availability and utilization of student services: - Academic advising - Career counseling - Personal counseling - Study skills development - Student social and extra-curricular activities • Community resources

Distribution of this explicit statement of institutional posture promotes understanding of the organization's direction and purpose among those groups whose support will be needed to achieve the stated goals.

Stage III - Resource Allocation

The purpose of the third stage of the cycle is to set specific, measurable objectives or targets for the size, scope, and outcomes of each of the institution's major programs and support programs. Five years is suggested as a planning period for this stage, though most organizations will find it desirable to employ a three-year planning horizon during the first few iterations of the cycle. Later on, periods of up to ten years may be covered with the amount of detail diminishing for the fifth through the tenth years of the period covered. Assuming the use of a five-year planning horizon, the task of setting objectives for each of the five years is combined with developing descriptions of the tactics to be used in achieving targets, schedules of planned activities and their estimated costs, and the measures to be used in evaluating progress. These descriptions constitute detailed operational plans for each program and for each administrative unit responsible for any part of a program. The first year of the multi-year operational plan provides the outline for constructing that year's budget, usually supplemented with some additional detail for revenues and expenditures. The annual budget is therefore a one-year slice of a multi-year operating plan. Because the budget alone lacks information on actions to be taken, results to be achieved, and outcomes to be reported, the accompanying descriptions of objectives and plans correct this deficiency.

The five-year forward plan and the annual budget are summarized for presentation to the board. The forward plan statements show the trustees how the organization intends to implement its chosen strategy and to what extent stated goals will be achieved during the period ahead. The annual budget serves not only as a financial plan for the coming year, but also, when accompanied by the forward plan, it shows the trustees what accomplishments will be sought with the associated expenditures.

Although the institution should distribute widely the statements of mission, goals, and strategies, forward operational plans and budgets do not require such distribution. However, each unit of the institution needs to have a clear understanding of its own approved objectives, plans, and budgets, as well as the targets and plans of related units. The combined effect of the resource allocation steps outlined above is to strengthen the personal commitment of division and department heads to attain agreed-upon objectives.

Stage IV - Evaluation

Answering the question of whether institutional objectives have been met, or, in the interim, whether satisfactory progress is being made toward meeting them is the primary purpose of the fourth stage of the planning cycle. In the event that final objectives or intermediate milestones are not being met, this stage provides for early identification of possible problem areas and facilitates the determination of corrective action.

Furthermore, the evaluation stage provides managers with an opportunity to report on their progress in relation to planned targets and to identify successes and shortfalls, both actual and anticipated. Evaluation steps should focus on elements of the organization's plans that are at least partly controllable in the near term by administrators responsible for the plans.

Evaluation also affords a basis for periodic reports to the board of trustees and enhances the board's understanding of the institution's requirements for support. The family of reports needed for monitoring and evaluating are collectively referred to as a management intelligence system and are described more fully in the next chapter.

Following the conclusion of the initial planning cycle, each stage should be repeated at specified intervals. For example, diagnostic steps would be carried out annually, although, after the first diagnosis, each update should not require extensive additions or revisions. In one instance, a college using this planning system found it possible to reduce slightly the size and scope of the planning data base each year and thus to focus its attention more heavily on a few issues of paramount concern.

The planning stage (determining mission and general goals) should be repeated annually, but major revisions usually should be necessary only at intervals of approximately five years. This is because only fundamental or unanticipated changes in the organization's environment or resources require a rethinking of mission or goals.

Resource allocation steps need to be repeated annually to incorporate changes in objectives, schedules, and estimated costs. After the first multi-year plan has been developed, the bulk of the effort is concentrated on two aspects of its contents: extending the plan forward an additional year and preparing a detailed budget for the coming year. Since the budget is merely an elaboration of one of the years already covered by the forward plan, its preparation does not require the intensive labor occasioned by budget-building in most organizations.

Reporting and evaluation should occur at quarterly intervals so that each administrator can keep the institution informed on progress in taking scheduled actions and on the results obtained in his or her area of responsibility. The review and discussion of evaluation reports serve as a basis for regular meetings of superior and subordinate administrators. In these meetings the focus should be on performance in relation to agreed-upon objectives. The reports and the meetings provide an opportunity for individual performance appraisal and supply information for decisions on merit increases and promotions.

BENEFITS OF THE SYSTEM

Seven primary benefits can result from implementation of the proposed planning and resource allocation system. First, the institution can make more effective use of its financial resources. Second, administrators gain a longer range perspective from which to make decisions. Third, the system provides for the identification of programs that need to be given priority in reallocating funds. Fourth, the institution can attract and develop capable administrators at all organizational levels. Fifth, the institution's fund-raising position is improved. Sixth, greater involvement on the part of trustees can be achieved. Finally, the participation of faculty and staff in planning and decision-making can be more carefully structured and, in some cases, increased.

More Effective Use of Resources

The identification of the mission and goals of an institution makes it possible to allocate resources in ways that lead more directly to the attainment of its goals. The test of effectiveness in resource use is whether expenditures lead to the desired outcomes. Thus, the determination of goals is the first step toward improving any organization's overall effectiveness.

In addition, the process of securing agreement among members of the college or university community on specific objectives can strengthen an individual manager's personal commitment to achieve planned results. Setting objectives and formulating plans also enhances communication and coordination among different parts of the organization. When communication is improved and commitments are strengthened, it is more likely that the efforts of key individuals will be directed to the most important elements of their responsibilities, and this in itself contributes to the effectiveness with which resources are expended.

Promoting a Longer Range Perspective

Managers frequently complain that they are kept from tasks of far-reaching significance by a constant barrage of immediate, day-to-day problems. This phenomenon stems in part from the fact that there is rarely a set of procedures in place to ensure that managers give adequate attention to the longer-range considerations involved in setting goals and objectives, choosing strategies and tactics, and evaluating their results against planned targets. As a result, issues are dealt with in order of their immediacy rather than in order of their importance. The proposed system facilitates the identification of major competitive and demographic developments in the institution's external environment, since these factors must be considered in formulating multiyear plans. The system also encourages administrators to view current problems as symptoms of underlying issues and promotes in-depth probing for what these issues might be and how they may be resolved. In this way, the system provides an opportunity to anticipate and perhaps avoid some problems.

Identification of Priority Programs

The planning process is generally the means by which an organization identifies those programs which promise the greatest future contributions to overall institutional growth and development. When such a program is identified at an early stage in its life cycle, resources can be allocated to it in order to accelerate its maturation. A new degree program, a new type of fund-raising activity, or an innovative approach to student financial aid are examples of actions which could produce higher-than-average payoffs if they are accorded sufficient priority to be funded adequately, even in a period of stable or declining levels of resource availability.

Moreover, most institutions are in the position of continuing to fund some programs whose period of usefulness is ending or has passed. These programs consume resources that could produce greater contributions to the university if invested in other activities. A systematic planning process permits identification of these obsolete programs and can also provide a strong rationale for phasing them out. The resources thereby freed can be reallocated to more promising areas.

Attracting and Developing Capable Managers

During the course of the planning process, middle-level administrators will have to learn to perform managerial tasks that may be quite new to them. Over a period of years, these individuals will become skilled in the use of new techniques of analysis, planning, and program evaluation. In the first few iterations of the cycle, however, the process should be viewed as an institution-wide management development and training project.

Once the managers are familiar with the system and it has been fully integrated into other administrative procedures, persons with a strong managerial orientation and an interest in developing their skills as managers are likely to be attracted to the organization on the basis of its reputation for innovative management practices. Thus, such a system can help an institution attract and retain capable administrators.

Improved Fund-Raising Posture

The most effective fund-raising is carried out by institutions able to communicate clearly a unique position among colleges and universities, to demonstrate tangible accomplishments, and to identify donors whose interests match the organization's mission and goals.

The first step in strengthening a fund-raising program is the formulation of a case statement or rationale for donors' support. However, unless the fund-raising case statement is also reflected in decisions on programs and services throughout the institution, fund-raisers find it difficult to explain persuasively why the donor's support is justified. When planning and resource allocation steps are in fact moving the organization in the directions expressed by the fund-raising case statement, administrators and trustees often find that their efforts to elicit support become more fruitful.

Since the case statement itself needs to articulate the institutional mission and goals, it is a logical by-product of the planning process.

Greater Trustee Involvement

A significant problem facing colleges and universities is the difficulty of securing active leadership on the part of governing boards. Trustees often lack sufficient familiarity with the institution for their decisions to be informed or constructive. This lack of knowledge in turn reflects an absence of close involvement in the deliberations leading to major policy recommendations.

An inadequate understanding of the proper roles of trustees, individually and as a group, frequently inhibits the development of effective board leadership. Chief among the duties and responsibilities of the governing board is, of course, selecting the institution's president and appraising his or her performance in office. The function next to these in importance is periodic review and approval of institutional objectives and plans.

Board members are understandably reluctant to become involved in the preparation of long-range plans, partly because of limits on the amount of time they have available for institutional governance and partly due to the large number of more routine items coming before the board for review and approval. When their role in planning is properly defined, however, it need not consume vast amounts of time. In this planning system the board's role is to study and act on carefully researched and brief reports on the results of each of the four stages of the planning and resource allocation cycle. In the process of reviewing these reports, trustees will acquire an adequate understanding of the institution's strengths and weaknesses, competitive position, mission and goals, and resource needs.

More Structured Faculty and Staff Participation

Participation in the planning process by members of the faculty and administrative staff has often been minimal or too narrowly circumscribed. This has been primarily because of the concern that if the number of people and organizational levels involved in planning were increased, the complexity of the process, and hence the amount of time required to complete each planning cycle, would rise substantially. One of the benefits of the proposed system is that faculty and staff participation, which is required to develop understanding of plans and commitment to achieving objectives, is carefully structured in each stage of the cycle. At the same time, there is clear recognition of the responsibility of top administrators for coordinating separate plan elements and for preparing final recommendations to the governing board.

PROCEDURES FOR PLANNING *3*

Implementing the planning and resource allocation cycle requires that certain tasks be performed in each of the four stages. Because the system's success depends on reaching conclusions and formulating recommendations at key points in the process, formats which present the required material most effectively are suggested.

STAGE I - DIAGNOSIS

The central task in this first stage is the compilation of a variety of types of information into a planning data base.

Assessing the present position of the institution requires two related types of analysis: first, the examination of trends in its internal educational and financial operations; and, second, determination of the present and future effects of developments occurring in the institution's external environment. These analyses are essential for preparing a planning agenda, or a list of problems and issues to be resolved in the course of the planning process.

To complete these analyses, a planning data base should be compiled. The purposes of the data base are to diagnose the present position of the institution, to identify actual and potential problem areas, to support subsequent planning efforts, and to provide a basis for monitoring progress after plans have been implemented. The elements of the data base will permit planners to answer specific questions about the organization's market position relative to its competitors, the strengths and weaknesses of its education programs, and its financial condition. Examples of the questions which need to be answered are listed in Exhibit III.

Construction of the data base requires two steps: first, the identification of planning questions or issues; and, second, the gathering of data to answer these questions and reach decisions on actions to be taken. These two elements must be carried out in tandem, since the data-gathering process usually identifies additional issues that need to be resolved. In gathering the data, planners should limit their concentration to critical problems, identifying at most ten major issues facing the institution and compiling only the data that is required to address these issues.

For example, one college identified five key questions to be answered during its first planning cycle:

1. What are the geographic, educational, and socio-economic characteristics of the market segment with the greatest potential for meeting our enrollment objectives, and how can we increase our share of this market?
2. How can we achieve a distinctive educational image that is appropriate to our market?
3. How can we increase overall instructional productivity so that faculty and staff compensation increases will not be translated fully into tuition increases that would impair our competitive position?
4. What are our capital requirements for the next five years and how can we meet them?
5. What can we do to improve the managerial skills of academic and support service administrators?

The planners at this college presented historical data and projections that defined the implications of these issues. They then prepared a report for circulation throughout the college before the planning cycle began.

After the data base has initially been compiled, responsibility should be assigned for its maintenance and improvement. The data base of information on marketing, operating, and financial issues should be updated annually and extended into new areas when additional questions are asked by planners. Identifying the most critical issues through use of a planning data base helps to focus concentration on those issues, whether they be marketing, operating, or financial.

Finally, the size of the data base should be reduced wherever possible by dropping less significant items. This step will facilitate its use by administrators throughout the institution.

STAGE II - PLANNING

The aim of this stage is to determine general goals and strategies. This is accomplished through the adoption of a mission statement, the identification of goals for major programs, the selection of strategies, and the assignment of priorities to programs.

Adoption of a Mission Statement

Within the framework of its legal charter, the institution should state its mission in broad, general terms. The statement should be worded so as to permit a maximum of flexibility in responding to changing circumstances. In order to be useful in guiding subsequent planning steps, however, the mission statement should define the range of services to be provided. These services should be defined in terms of geographic service areas, whether local, regional, or national, and also in terms of target groups in the population. The definition of services and client groups should be linked to findings and conclusions drawn from previous diagnostic tasks and may require some further analysis of trends and developments in the institution's external environment.

The mission statement should be brief, no more than a few paragraphs, and, like a fund-raising case statement, should be written in nontechnical language so that it will be readily understandable to students, alumni, donors, funding agencies, and others.

Identification of Goals for Major Programs

Within the context of the mission statement, goals should be formulated for each major program and service. These goals will therefore need to be stated in fairly general, nonquantitative terms. They should be designed to remain valid over a period of at least five to ten years and should consequently be addressed to

---

DIAGNOSTIC QUESTIONS TO BE ANSWERED

I. Marketing Profile: What Is Our Market Niche?
   - What are our markets and market segments?
   - What is our market share in each segment?
   - Who are our competitors?
   - What are the demographic trends and projections for each market segment?
   - What effects will these developments have on our enrollment?
   - What are the key competitive factors in our markets? Price? Program? Location?
   - Do prospective students in our market segments correctly perceive our net effective price (after aid awards)?

II. Operating Profile: How Effective Are Our Educational Programs?
   - What are attrition rates in each program and at each student level?
   - What results are each of our programs producing?
   - What are our graduates doing in their fields of study or related fields?
   - How do our programs compare with those offered by other institutions in degree productivity, graduate productivity, instructional productivity, and cost productivity?
   - How well is our physical plant and equipment base utilized?
   - In covering their functional responsibilities, how productive are our managers, relative to their counterparts in other institutions?

III. Financial Profile: What Is Our Financial Condition?
- What are revenues and expenditures, total and per-student, by function and program?
- What is the extent of dependence on each revenue component?
- Are auxiliary enterprises self-financing?
- How good has our investment management performance been?
- What is the status of our financial control systems and procedures?
- What is our indebtedness? Debt capacity? Debt service coverage ratio?
- How adequately are capital needs being met, including major maintenance, renovation, and replacement projects?

market trends and public needs that are themselves expected to be relatively durable, even if not highly predictable in a quantitative sense.

Goals should be developed first for education and public service programs; then, after these have been approved, for support activities. A college or university without separate professional schools should prepare goal statements covering the following educational, research, and public service program areas:
- Undergraduate general education
- Undergraduate professional education programs, by field of study
- Graduate and research programs, by field of study
- Nondegree and other continuing education programs
- Extension and other public service activities

In a university with separate colleges and professional schools, each separately organized entity should formulate goals for the above categories of programs.

Goal statements should then be prepared for the following central and school-level support activities:
- Academic and student services such as student recruitment, financial aid, libraries, academic records, student activities, and career counseling and placement
- Public and alumni relations, publications, and public information
- Fund-raising programs
- Business and financial services such as personnel and labor relations, physical plant management, purchasing, treasury functions, and investment management
- Auxiliary enterprises, including residences, bookstores, food services, and conferences

Operating goals for these areas should be brief and nontechnical and should be stated largely in terms of desired outcomes or results to be achieved by each program. While these outcomes or results do not need to be directly measurable, they should be described clearly enough so that they can be measured at least indirectly. During the resource allocation stage, these goal statements will need to be translated into measureable objectives. If goals are defined in terms of end results or desired outcomes, then objectives can be set to indicate how much of the goal is to be realized within a specific time period. Then, in the evaluation stage, one can determine whether or not adequate progress is being made toward the achievement of stated goals.

It may prove necessary to revise goal statements several times to achieve coordination and consistency among related educational, research, public service, and support programs. This is particularly important during the first few iterations of the planning cycle, when program interrelationships are being analyzed explicitly for perhaps the first time.

Selection of Strategies and Assignment of Priorities

Once goals have been set for each program, a strategic approach to attaining that goal can be specified. Matters of strategy will already have been given implicit consideration, since the approval of goals is based on some understanding, however general, that the stated goals are feasible. At this point, the task is to describe how, over a period of years, the organization will acquire and use the resources needed to reach the goal.

Strategies should be viewed as relatively durable arrangements, sustained over minimum periods of three to five years and not subject to substantial interim changes. This stability is necessary in that strategies will generally involve complex combinations of commitments of physical facilities, administrative staff, and specialized faculty that cannot be either acquired or re-directed in fewer than two years, and sometimes not even in much longer periods. Moreover, the evaluation of the effectiveness of programs often cannot be made without at least three to five years' implementation experience.

In selecting strategies, an institution should begin by analyzing the strengths and weaknesses of the strategic approach currently used in each of its programs. Where a strategy appears to be ineffective, a list of alternatives can be developed and the feasibility and probable consequences of each alternative strategy can be assessed. There may also be inconsistencies or conflicts between strategies being considered for separate programs; further revisions may therefore be necessary before strategic decisions can be finalized.

When strategies have been chosen, the institution should assign relative priorities to major programs based on the potential contribution of each to the overall mission of the organization. Priorities should also reflect the risks involved and the relative feasibility of chosen strategies. For example, high-risk strategies would only be given top priority when their potential payoffs were also high. Low-risk strategies would receive low priorities when even full achievement of the stated goal would make only a modest contribution to fulfilling the overall mission of the institution.

A suggested format for displaying the results of the planning stage (program goals, strategies, and priorities) is shown in Exhibit IV. This display facilitates a final review of decisions on program goals, strategies, and priorities, and provides an additional opportunity to ensure that the program selected for continued funding include only those with feasible strategies. Moreover, planners should balance high-risk programs by including some with lower levels of risk. In assignments of relative priorities, there should be a balance of high- and low-priority programs so that preference in allocating resources can be given to the former category without the need for continuing debate over matters of risk, payoff, and feasibility.

At the conclusion of the planning stage, a report should be prepared setting forth and explaining all recommended program decisions. This report should be submitted to the governing

Exhibit IV

FORMAT FOR SUMMARIZING PROGRAM GOALS, STRATEGIES, AND PRIORITIES

Program Name: _____

Goals	Current Trends And Competitive Factors	Proposed Strategic Approach	Estimated Resource Requirements And Sources of Support	Potential Level of Contribution to Institutional Mission	Recommended Priority

board for its examination and action. If the board's review indicates the need for further consideration in any or all areas, then the planning steps described above should be repeated. When the report is approved by the board, the institution may proceed to the resource allocation stage.

STAGE III - RESOURCE ALLOCATION

At this stage, general goals and strategies will be converted into specific objectives, operating plans, and budgets. This conversion is accomplished through the following tasks:
- Set measurable objectives for all programs
- Develop five-year schedule of plans for achieving objectives
- Prepare annual budget with detailed action plans and associated costs

Set Measurable Objectives

In all programs for which general goals have been formulated, specific objectives should be set for each year of the planning period. These objectives, viewed as targets, should be stated in such a way that the extent to which they are realized can be measured, either quantitatively or judgmentally. If the goal cannot be translated directly into quantifiable objectives, then the objectives should be defined in terms of measurable variables that are, at least indirectly, related to the goal.

For example, if, among its goals, an institution seeks to build and maintain an enrollment that makes optimum use of its physical, managerial, and instructional resources, then two of its objectives for a five-year period might be to enroll annually 2,400 new freshmen and 600 transfer students and to reduce the attrition rate by two percentage points each year. Choosing the figures for these objectives would be based on careful analyses of institutional capacity, student demand, market and competitive trends, and factors contributing to student attrition.

As another example, a university with the goal of providing a graduate management program of recognized high quality within its geographic service area might set objectives for each of the following variables:
- Applicants per place
- Academic and professional experience profile of entering students
- Placement offers per graduate
- Average starting salary of graduates

Utilizing these and other variables, progress in realizing goals then could be monitored both absolutely and relative to its identified competitors in the same service area.

During the first iteration of the planning cycle, a five-year time horizon should be employed. Later, this period can be extended to periods of as long as ten years, particularly when large capital expenditures are being considered or when the institution is considering such issues as opening or closing a separate campus, merging with another institution, or launching a major capital campaign.

A format for the conversion of general goals into specific objectives is illustrated for two goals in Exhibit V. Exhibit VI then shows how several different objectives for an existing academic program or a proposed new program would be presented. A narrative statement should be attached to Exhibit VI explaining how goals were converted into objectives and how objectives were formulated for each year of the planning period. Support program objectives should be developed and justified in similar fashion. Exhibit VII presents a suggested format for student recruitment program objectives. (See pp. 37-39.)

When all units have completed initial work on objectives, these should be reviewed on a program-by-program basis, compiled, and examined as an integrated whole before being approved by the executive team and before consideration is given to developing detailed operating plans. This step enables the institution to ensure coordination and consistency among the objectives of all educational and support programs. As a result of this review, additional revisions may be needed before objectives are finally approved.

Develop Operating Plans

Once trustees and top executives have reached agreement on final objectives, the institution should develop detailed operating plans. This step involves the selection of tactics: what actions will be taken, by whom, with what frequency and costs, and for what results. In selecting tactics, managers should give primary consideration to issues of feasibility, to ensure that chosen methods are within the limits of available financial and personnel resources, since these constraints are often relatively inflexible in the near term. Discussions of proposed tactics should focus on how the recommended actions will lead to accomplishment of the stated objective.

Managers can begin by generating a list of possible approaches and assessing estimated costs and probable consequences of each. By ranking each of these approaches in order of feasibility or cost-effectiveness, the managers can determine the logical final selections. This method encourages innovation since it requires administrators to consider alternatives to existing tactics.

After tactics have been agreed upon, managers can proceed to develop schedules of actions to be taken. Exhibits VIII through X (see pp. 40-45) present suggested formats for displaying plans for academic and support programs. In preparing these operating plans, managers should demonstrate how the proposed activities will contribute to the attainment of approved objectives. Among the questions to be asked during this phase are the following:

- Is there evidence that the proposed activities have in the past been effective in achieving the stated objectives, at this institution or another?
- Have related activities been linked together in a coordinated plan?
- Are cost estimates both realistic and feasible?
- How reasonable are the relationships between promised benefits and estimated costs?

During this stage of the cycle, top administrators should continue to refine their judgments about the institution's most promising programs of instruction, public service, and research so that resources can be shifted into these programs during the annual budgeting process.

Prepare an Annual Budget

The final task of the resource allocation stage is to prepare a detailed financial plan or budget for the coming year, the first of the five years covered by the operating plan. This financial plan corresponds closely to the annual budget prepared by most colleges and universities. It differs, however, in that it has been preceded by the development of explicit statements of objectives, tactics, and action plans. Thus budget preparation can be carried out in a more efficient and meaningful fashion. Most organizations attempt to force the budget preparation process to include planning and resource allocation functions for which this process is, by itself, ill-suited. As a result, budget-building tasks consume inordinate amounts of managerial time and energy without contributing significantly to the development of agreements on continuing or new program objectives and plans.

Under the system proposed here, the process of developing the operating budget is part of the overall planning process, but represents only a slight elaboration on the decisions made in developing five-year operating plans. As a result, more of the time set aside for budget preparation can be used in refining estimates of revenues and expenditures, thus contributing to greater accuracy in forecasts and allowing greater precision in financial management.

Normally, the first-year section of the approved operating plan would serve as the basis for the annual budget, with additional detail added where necessary to meet the requirements of funding agencies and internal financial control procedures. However, special circumstances or unexpected developments might necessitate modification of the first-year's plan in preparing the budget. For example, new developments in federal or state student aid programs might require that institutional scholarship budgets be adjusted. As a result, the implementation of certain plans might be accelerated or postponed.

The budget preparation process should include the development of general assumptions and guidelines based on prior planning and resource allocation decisions; determination of institution-wide priorities and critical tasks for the year ahead; estimates of changes in total and individual program enrollments based on year-to-date recruitment results; and forecasts of fund availability for staff additions, promotions, and compensation increases.

Each division and unit of the institution should be provided with up-to-date information on its past results, prior-year expenditures, year-to-date spending, and current budget balances. Budget requests then can be constructed, each to be accompanied by a narrative statement setting forth the following:

- Operating objectives to be attained during the budget year (expressed either as end results of programs or as implementation actions to be taken)
- Relationship of these objectives to five-year objectives
- Quarterly or semi-annual milestones for measuring progress toward objectives
- Alternative spending and activity levels under lower and higher levels of available resources

Each division, school, or college should review its own budget requests first. Then all should be compiled and reviewed centrally on an institution-wide basis. These reviews may result in substantial revisions, particularly during initial iterations of the cycle and during times of changing resource levels.

Following completion of the budget preparation step, the governing board should receive a summary report setting forth major institutional objectives, operating plans, and the budget for the coming year. This report should be reviewed and either approved or returned for further consideration. The trustees' approval encompasses all three components; thus, the budget will not be approved unless the trustees agree with the objectives and plans which the budget is designed to support.

STAGE IV - EVALUATION

An institution uses the evaluation stage to monitor the execution of approved plans and to reward managers appropriately for their achievements. Three key words that succinctly describe this stage are assign, measure, and reward.

Assign Responsibility for Attaining Objectives

Following governing board approval of objectives, plans, and the annual budget, each individual manager should be assigned specific responsibility for implementing plans and for accomplishing those elements of the overall objectives that fall within his or her area. For each element of the plan, individual commitments should be secured from unit leaders, including faculty department and division heads.

If more than one administrator is responsible for program plans that embrace two or more separate organizational units, agreement must be reached among all affected managers.

Measure Performance Against Plans

The measurement and evaluation of performance, as opposed to spending, is not an established tradition among most institutions of higher education. Moreover, in many organizations, there appears to be substantial resistance to focusing directly on the performance of programs, departments, divisions, or schools. Nevertheless, certain needs cannot be met without measuring performance:

- To determine if plans are being implemented as intended by the governing board and administrators, particularly in organizations too large for the president and his or her staff to be directly involved in day-to-day administration
- To indicate the need for appropriate action should im-

plementation fall behind schedule
- To determine the extent to which planned activities are producing the results originally predicted when operating plans were drawn up
- To ensure coordination among organizational units responsible for related plan elements
- To highlight the need for periodic changes in objectives, plans, organizational structures, or individual assignments
- To facilitate meaningful progress reports to the governing board, funding agencies, and others interested in the welfare of the institution
- To guide future planning and resource allocation efforts

These needs can be met through the use of an integrated family of reports on operating performance. Collectively, these reports are referred to as a "management intelligence system." In contrast to the narrow fiscal focus of most operating reports, the management intelligence system proposed here has three distinctive capabilities. First, in addition to covering budgetary matters, it reports on matters relating to annual objectives, interim targets, and implementation activities. Second, the system focuses on exceptions to planned results in order to curtail the time required to develop the reports and to limit their length. Third, the system disseminates information to all managers who are executing and administering operating plans.

Each organizational unit prepares a monthly report setting forth any favorable or unfavorable divergence from planned actions and results. This report should describe the causes and possible consequences of any such divergences and should suggest follow-up steps to be taken. Senior managers review and use the reports as the basis for summary reports to the president. The top executives of the organization should receive reports covering only the most significant variances from plans; that is, those variances which require action by top management in order to resolve problems or to take advantage of opportunities for improvement. In addition, the governing board should receive a summary at least once each quarter, with more frequent reports going to the board's executive committee.

At a minimum, operating reports should cover plans made and results achieved in student recruitment and admissions, academic programs, fund-raising, and financial operations.

Illustrative examples of the suggested format and content of operating reports are presented in Exhibits XI through XIV.

(Text continues on page 58.)

Exhibit V

FORMAT FOR CONVERSION OF GOALS INTO OBJECTIVES

Goal	Five-Year Objectives					Near-Term Implication	Responsibility Level
	1980-81	1981-82	1982-83	1983-84	1984-85		
	A - Total Enrollment						
Total Enrollment At Capacity	9,200	9,400	9,500	9,500	9,500	2,235 new students entering in September of 1980 (a)	Vice President for Academic Affairs
	B - Gift Income (Millions) (b)						
Maintain Stable Financial Condition	$12.8	$13.9	$15.2	$16.5	$18.0	12 per cent increase over 1978-79	Vice President for External Relations

(a) Assumes 15 per cent annual attrition from 1978-79 to 1980-81.
(b) Excludes government grants.

Exhibit VI

FORMAT FOR ACADEMIC PROGRAM OBJECTIVES
Planned Years 1980-81 Through 1984-85

Academic Division: _____
Program Name: _____

Goal Category	Actual		Estimated		Planned		
	1977-78	1978-79	1979-80	1980-81	1981-82	1982-83	1983-84	1984-85

1. Degrees Conferred

2. Certificates Awarded (a)

3. Other (b)

Note: Attach a narrative statement of program objectives; relate objectives to program goals; indicate what graduates will do following completion of program; discuss feasibility of objectives.

(a) Represents adult and continuing (nondegree) education programs.
(b) Includes public and community service projects, research and consulting, and other program goals.

Exhibit VII

FORMAT FOR SUPPORT PROGRAM OBJECTIVES
Planned Years 1980-81 Through 1984-85

Support Area: *Academic Services*
Support Program: *Student Recruitment*

Goal Category	Actual		Estimated		Planned			
	1977-78	1978-79	1979-80	1980-81	1981-82	1982-83	1983-84	1984-85
1. Entering Students (a)								
Commuting freshmen								
Resident freshmen								
Commuting transfers								
Resident transfers								
Total								

Note: Attach a narrative statement relating objectives to goals; discuss feasibility and justification of proposed objectives.
What factors might prevent their being attained? What should be done to enhance or promote the prospects of success?

(a) All terms.

Exhibit VIII

FORMAT FOR ACADEMIC PROGRAM PLANS
Planned Years 1980-81 Through 1984-85

Academic Division: _____

Program Name: _____

Category (a)	Actual		Esti-mated		Planned		
	1977-78	1978-79	1979-80	1980-81	1981-82	1982-83	1983-84	1984-85

1. Approved Objectives
   Degrees conferred
   Certificates awarded
   Other

2. Number of Student
   Majors (b)
   Lower Division
   Upper Division
   Graduate

Exhibit VIII (continued)

Category (a)	Actual		Esti-mated	Planned				
	1977-78	1978-79	1979-80	1980-81	1981-82	1982-83	1983-84	1984-85
3. Credit Hours Generated (c)								
Lower Division								
Upper Division								
Graduate								
4. Resources Required								
Number of faculty								
Other (explain)								
Total Cost								

(a) Attach narrative explaining and justifying all entries.
(b) This program only.
(c) This division only.

Exhibit IX

FORMAT FOR A SUPPORT PROGRAM PLAN: STUDENT RECRUITMENT

Planned Years 1980-81 Through 1984-85

Support Area: *Academic Services*
Support Program: *Student Recruitment*

Category (a)	Actual		Esti-mated			Planned		
	1977-78	1978-79	1979-80	1980-81	1981-82	1982-83	1983-84	1984-85
1. Approved Objectives								
Entering freshmen								
Entering transfers								
Total								
2. Recruitment Plan (b)								
Number of schools covered								
Number of prospects contacted								
Other techniques/activities								
Number of inquiries								
Number of applicants								
Number accepted								

Exhibit IX (continued)

Category (a)	Actual		Esti-mated	Planned			
	1977-78	1978-79	1979-80	1980-81	1981-82	1982-83	1983-84	1984-85
3. Resources Required								
Staff (number and cost)								
Travel cost								
Other (type and cost)								
Total Cost								

(a) Attach narrative explaining and justifying all entries.

(b) Show details in supporting schedules.

Exhibit X

FORMAT FOR A SUPPORT PROGRAM PLAN: VOLUNTARY SUPPORT
Planned Years 1980-81 Through 1984-85

Support Area: *External Relations*
Support Program: *Voluntary Support*

Category (a)	Actual		Esti-mated	Planned				
	1977-78	1978-79	1979-80	1980-81	1981-82	1982-83	1983-84	1984-85
1. Approved Objectives (b)								
Capital gifts								
Operating gifts								
Total								
2. Activity Plan								
Personal solicitations								
Group meetings								
Mailings								
Other								

Exhibit X (continued)

Category (a)	Actual		Esti-mated	Planned				
	1977-78	1978-79	1979-80	1980-81	1981-82	1982-83	1983-84	1984-85
3. Resources Required								
Number and type of staff								
Staff cost								
Other costs								
Total Cost								

(a) Attach narrative explaining and justifying all entries.
(b) Show number and dollar amount of gifts by source.

Exhibit XI

MANAGEMENT INTELLIGENCE SYSTEM

Support Program: *Admissions* Date: _____

Subprogram: *Freshman Recruitment* Period Covered: _____

Monthly Admissions Report

Sources	Targets		This Year		Last Year		Comments
				Year To Date			
	Commuting	Resident	Commuting	Resident	Commuting	Resident	
In-State							
Region I							
Region II							
Regions III and IV							
Regions V and VI							
Other States							
Illinois							
Kansas							
Missouri							
Oklahoma							
Texas							
Other							
International							

Exhibit XI (continued)

Monthly Admissions Report (Cont'd)

Sources	Actions Planned (a)		Progress To Date	Comments
	Action	Key Dates		
In-State				
Region I				
Region II				
Regions III and IV				
Regions V and VI				
Other States				
Illinois				
Kansas				
Missouri				
Oklahoma				
Texas				
Other				
International				

(a) Focus on key elements of approved operating plan.

Exhibit XII

MANAGEMENT INTELLIGENCE SYSTEM

Program: *Academic*

Date: _____

Period Covered: _____

Quarterly Academic Program Summary

College/Division	Actions Planned (a)		Progress To Date	Comments
	Action	Key Dates		
Business Administration				
Education				
Fine Arts and Humanities				
Natural Science and Mathematics				
Social Sciences				
Adult and Continuing Education				

(a) Focus on major elements of approved operating plan.

Exhibit XII (continued)

Semester Productivity Summary

College/Division	Credit-Hours Taught		FTE Faculty		Instructional Expenditures		Credit-Hours Per FTE		Cost Per Credit-Hour		Comments (a)
	Plan	Actual	Plan	Actual	Plan	Actual	Plan	Actual	Plan	Actual	
Business Administration											
Education											
Fine Arts and Humanities											
Natural Science and Mathematics											
Social Sciences											
Adult and Continuing Education											
Total											

(a) Explain variances between planned and actual results and describe follow-up actions being taken or considered.

Exhibit XIII

MANAGEMENT INTELLIGENCE SYSTEM

Support Program: *Voluntary Support*

Subprogram: *Annual Giving*

Date: _____

Period Covered: _____

Monthly Giving Report Summary

Sources	Targets		This Year		Last Year		Comments (a)
	Number of Gifts	Amount	Number	Amount	Number	Amount	
Trustees							
Alumni							
Other Individuals							
Church							
Foundations							
Corporations							
Other Sources							
Total							

(a) Explain variances between planned and actual results, and indicate follow-up actions being taken or considered.

Exhibit XIII (continued)

Monthly Giving Report Summary (Cont'd)

Sources	Actions Planned		Progress to Date	Comments
	Action	Key Dates		
Trustees				
Alumni				
Other Individuals				
Churches				
Foundations				
Corporations				
Other Sources				
Total				

Exhibit XIV

MANAGEMENT INTELLIGENCE SYSTEM

Support Program: *Finance*

Date: _____

Period Covered: _____

Monthly Budget Summary: *Revenues*

Source	Full Year Results		This Period		This Year		Last Year		Comments (a)
	Budget	Esti-mated	Budget	Actual	Budget	Actual	Budget	Actual	
						Year-To-Date			
Tuition And Fees									
Endowment									
Gifts									
Government Grants									
Miscellaneous									
Total									

(a) Explain variances between budgeted and actual revenues and indicate steps being taken or considered to eliminate unfavorable variances.

Exhibit XIV (continued)

Monthly Budget Summary: Revenues (Cont'd)

Sources	Actions Planned (a)		Progress To Date	Comments
	Action	Key Dates		
Tuition and Fees				
Endowment				
Gifts				
Government Grants				
Miscellaneous				
Total				

(a) Focus on key elements of approved operating plan for this support program.

Exhibit XIV (continued)

MANAGEMENT INTELLIGENCE SYSTEM

Support Program: *Finance*

Date: _____
Period Covered: _____

Monthly Budget Summary: Expenditures

Unit	Full Year Results		This Period		Year-To-Date					Comments (a)
					This Year		Last Year			
	Budget	Esti-mated	Budget	Actual	Budget	Actual	Budget	Actual		
Top Administration										
Board of Trustees										
President's Office										
Finance										
Business Office										
Plant Maintenance and Operation										

Exhibit XIV (continued)

Unit	Full Year Results Budget	Full Year Results Esti-mated	This Period Budget	This Period Actual	Year-To-Date This Year Budget	Year-To-Date This Year Actual	Year-To-Date Last Year Budget	Year-To-Date Last Year Actual	Comments (a)
Institutional Relations									
Development Office									
Public Information Office									
Academic Affairs									
Vice President's Office									
Student Services									
Academic Divisions									
Other									
Total									

(a) Explain variances between budgeted and actual expenditures, and indicate steps being taken or considered to eliminate negative variances.

Exhibit XIV (continued)

Monthly Budget Summary: Expenditures (Cont'd)

Unit	Actions Planned (a)		Progress To Date	Comments
	Action	Key Dates		
Top Administration				
Board of Trustees				
President's Office				
Finance				
Business Office				
Plant Maintenance and Operations				
Institutional Relations				
Development Office				
Public Information Office				
Academic Affairs				
Vice President's Office				
Student Services				
Academic Divisions				

(a) Focus on key elements of approved operating plan for this support program.

Exhibit XIV (continued)
Support Program: *Finance*
Subprogram: *Auxiliary Enterprises*

Monthly Budget Summary: Revenues And Expenditures

Unit	This Period			Year-To-Date			Full Year Net Results (a)		Comments
	Revenues	Expenditures	Net(a)	Revenues	Expenditures	Net(a)	Budget	Estimated	
Food Service									
Residences									
Bookstores									
Conferences									
Other									
Total									

(a) Net contribution to institutional overhead.

Reward Individual Managers

The final task in the resource allocation process is to ensure that the performance of individual managers is evaluated and that they are compensated in accordance with the degree of effectiveness they demonstrate in implementing plans and achieving approved objectives. This strengthens their commitment to realizing institutional goals and increases their involvement in the planning process.

The performance appraisal system should cover at least those positions reporting directly to the institution's chief executive officer, as well as the next level of administrative staff. For example, in a college of 5,000 students, these two administrative levels would encompass approximately 25 positions. Each manager would initially prepare an appraisal of his or her own record of accomplishment for the previous year. The manager would then submit this appraisal for review and discussion to the immediate supervisor after which the supervisor would submit a recommendation on the manager's compensation to the next level of management.

There are several ways of linking compensation increases to managerial performance. One feasible approach for nonprofit organizations relates the individual's salary increase to the results of the performance appraisal. For example, if the average salary increase for all eligible managers were 8 per cent, then individual increases could range from a minimum of no increase to a maximum of 20 per cent, excluding increases resulting from promotions or position reclassifications. Assuming that performance was appraised at quarterly intervals, a manager demonstrating outstanding performance might be awarded five percentage points each quarter toward an end-of-year salary increase. At the beginning of the following year, the manager's salary would be raised 20 per cent. Another approach would be to pay an annual bonus, figured as a percentage of the manager's salary. The advantage of this approach is that incentive or merit compensation is not made part of the recipient's base salary. This separation helps to preserve the integrity of the institution's administrative salary structure. Other approaches can be employed, of course; however, the important principles are first, direct linkage between performance appraisal and compensation, and, second, frequent appraisals and notification of rewards.

ORGANIZATION FOR PLANNING 4

Recommendations on the assignment of responsibilities for carrying out required planning and resource allocation tasks are generally applicable to the entire process, and specifically to each of the four stages of the planning cycle. Any given institution might have to modify some details, but the suggestions discussed in this chapter are directed to the overall planning process.

GENERAL RECOMMENDATIONS

The governing board of the institution should review and approve, at least in summary form, all statements of mission, goals, and objectives. Prior to submission to the trustees, however, planning materials should be studied and approved by the president and the executive officers reporting directly to the president. The executive officers should, as a team, oversee and direct the preparation and implementation of the entire planning process, and the president, as the institution's chief administrative officer, should be accountable to the board for the performance of this team. These assignments of responsibility are intended to make it clear to all participants that planning is an aspect of line administration, rather than a staff function.

While the executive team may delegate substantial elements of its planning duties, this group should personally review and approve (or return for further consideration) all plans developed at lower levels of the organization prior to transmitting them to the board of trustees for final review and action. Top executives should each provide active leadership in the formulation of plans in their individual areas of responsibility. The provost or chief academic officer should guide the efforts of deans and other academic program directors in preparing plans for ongoing and new instruction and research programs, academic support functions, and student services. The top administrator for fundraising and public relations should lead staff members in developing plans for voluntary support, alumni affairs and relationships with governmental agencies and the general public. Plans for financial management, personnel administration, physical plant operations, and auxiliary enterprises should be compiled under the direction of the chief financial officer of the institution. The role of the executive team is to guide and coordinate planning activities in the separate organizational units to ensure that proposals ultimately submitted are grounded in a common understanding of mission and goals and are mutually consistent in their consequences for the institution.

STAGE I - DIAGNOSIS

The president should assign to a staff assistant responsibility for compiling a data base of planning information covering external developments and recent trends in the educational and financial operations of the institution. In larger colleges, the institutional research office could perform this function. In universities with separate graduate and professional schools, the dean of each college or school should assign responsibility for preparing a planning data base covering external and internal trends affecting that unit. Throughout the balance of this chapter, the discussion assumes that planning is carried out on an institution-wide basis and does not describe the additional arrangements that need to be made for each separate college or school within a large university. However, the adaptations required for such units represent extensions of the process outlined in this chapter. The deans of separate schools within a university repeat with their immediate staff the tasks here assigned to the chief executive officer of the institution.

The topics listed in Exhibit II, Chapter 1, provide a starting point for constructing an initial data base. This information would also be used for other purposes such as general institutional research, responses to external surveys, and government and foundation proposals.

When the planning data has been compiled and summarized, either centrally or within each separate school, brief reports on major trends and developments should be distributed to all managers who will be involved in the planning and resource allocation process. The summary report should be studied carefully by all members of the top executive team. The president should then arrange to meet with the executive team members, preferably away from the daily office pressure. This meeting should focus on the past performance of the institution, its outlook and prospects, and the impact of developments in its external environment. Among the outcomes of this session should be agreement on what critical issues face the organization and require resolution during the forthcoming planning cycle.

From this meeting should come a statement of critical issues, operating trends, and external developments: a report that could be drafted for the team by a staff assistant. This report is to be circulated, in draft form, within the top executive group for comment. As the final step in this part of the cycle, the team prepares a diagnostic report based on the above draft and revisions and submits it to the board of trustees for review and approval.

While the work of the diagnostic stage should be carried out in a relatively concentrated manner by a small group of top managers, as described above, the distribution of the final diagnostic report should be fairly broad, including all academic and non-academic administrators who will be directly involved in subsequent planning and resource allocation tasks.

STAGE II - PLANNING

In contrast to the work of the diagnostic stage, planning steps should involve the participation of a larger proportion of the management group. The executive team should take the lead in preparing preliminary statements of mission and goals. These statements should be circulated among all top managers, division and department heads, and academic program directors for their reactions and suggestions. The results of this process should be incorporated into final versions of mission and goal statements.

In defining and evaluating strategic alternatives, academic and support service managers should work closely with members of the executive team. While top administrators have primary responsibility for deciding on program goals that are consistent with the overall mission of the institution, program managers are in the best position to propose strategic approaches to attaining those goals and to make recommendations as to which strategies should be employed.

If major questions of strategy need to be resolved, the president or a member of the executive team should appoint a small task force of managers familiar with the program or programs under study. The role of these task forces would be to explore key issues, analyze alternatives, and make recommendations to the executive team. However, the executive team, subject to the endorsement of the president and the final approval of the governing board, retains responsibility for the final decisions on programs to be added, modified, or discontinued, on relative program priorities, and on the strategy to be followed with each program.

STAGE III - RESOURCE ALLOCATION

The resource allocation process should take place largely at the operating level of the organization, at which point department and division directors and support service administrators are most familiar with the details of education and support programs. The president initiates the work of this stage, however, by distributing a brief report outlining the final results of the planning stage. This report should contain guidelines for developing objectives, operating plans, and budgets, as well as suggested formats for presenting written materials.

As statements of objectives and plans are prepared at the lowest administrative levels, they should be reviewed at each higher level, compiled into groups of related programs and services, checked for consistency, and either approved or returned for additions, deletions, or modifications. The executive team should make a final review before operating plans and the annual budget are submitted to the board of trustees for their approval.

STAGE IV - EVALUATION

Each member of the top executive team should personally direct the process of assigning responsibility for executive operating plans in individual areas of responsibility. This step involves negotiations at each administrative level to gain agreement on the results that are to be obtained and the schedule for their accomplishment. This process should follow a top-to-bottom pattern until managers at the lowest levels of the organization have made commitments to achieve specific targets.

Primary responsibility for measuring performance against plans rests with the division, department, and support service directors. At regular intervals, each manager should prepare a brief narrative report describing progress being made in relation to agreed-upon annual objectives and interim targets. Their reports should be supplemented by the operations of the management intelligence system outlined in the previous chapter.

The chief academic officer and the registrar should, at quarterly or semiannual intervals, jointly prepare and distribute to division and department heads reports covering enrollment, degrees conferred, instructional productivity, and other areas in which specific objectives have been set. The top business officer should oversee the development of monthly revenue and expenditure reports for use by division and department heads in monitoring their financial operations. The chief development officer should, with his staff, design an integrated set of reports that summarize activities and achievements in the areas of fund-raising and government grants. In turn, division and department heads should use this information to monitor their own performance and to report quarterly on any divergences from plans. In such critical areas as student recruitment and fund-raising, a monthly reporting interval would be optimal. The entire executive team should review all reports on a regular basis. Individual managers should bring evidence of actual or potential problems in their areas to the attention of this team as soon as possible and in a form indicating both the need for action and the nature of the action required. The executive team thus should place reviews of performance reports on their agenda at least once a month.

IMPLEMENTATION OF THE SYSTEM

5

Successful implementation of the proposed planning and resource allocation system depends on five factors. These include the clarity of existing assignments of administrative responsibility, the degree of participation by trustees, the quality of teamwork among executives, the availability of training programs for academic and support service administrators, and the timetable for implementation. These factors will need to be considered prior to and during the implementation of the planning process.

STRENGTHENING ADMINISTRATIVE ORGANIZATION

Effective planning and resource allocation are heavily dependent on the existence of a soundly structured administrative organization. Certain characteristics of organizational structure particularly affect the system's functioning. For instance, it is necessary to have related programs and services grouped together in divisions and departments to promote coordination and to simplify channels of communication. At all organizational levels, each manager's span of control (the number of positions reporting directly to him or her) should be broad enough to utilize fully his or her skills and talents, but not so broad as to frustrate effective leadership and control.

If a manager is responsible for two or more separate programs, multiple reporting channels should be eliminated or, at least, kept to a minimum. At each level in the structure, balanced administrative workloads facilitate the promotion of equity, the avoidance of bottlenecks, and provision of a sound basis for compensation schedules. Administrative duties and responsibilities of each position in the structure should be clearly defined and fully understood by all superiors, subordinates, and closely related positions. Overlapping responsibilities and duplication of efforts should be eliminated by redefining or reassigning roles and tasks.

To ensure that these characteristics are reflected in actual practice, it is usually necessary to examine the organizational structure closely at regular intervals, usually every two or three years. Weaknesses generally result from natural growth or decline in programs and services or from changes in work methods or procedures that have led to new managerial requirements. Thus, periodic surveys of responsibilities and administrative practices can uncover problems that need to be corrected.

For example, expansion in the number and variety of instructional and administrative applications for computer systems has caused major growth in the workload of computer centers. Because of this growth, institutions have had to review the organizational location of the data processing function and the type of manager needed to direct it. Other areas in which functional and workload changes are creating changes in organizational structure include labor relations, adult and continuing education, student recruitment and financial aid, affirmative action programs, contract research, and governmental relations.

Finally, no matter how clearly organizational relationships have been defined, these definitions are of little value unless the incumbent of each office possesses an accurate understanding of his or her duties and responsibilities. Since staff turnover occurs at a rate that is normally greater than the rate of organizational changes, active training programs in each division and department ensure that all incumbents share a common understanding of their own and others' assignments.

SECURING TRUSTEE INVOLVEMENT

The proposed planning and resource allocation process is designed to secure significant participation by the governing board of the institution. Consequently, the process can be fully institutionalized only when trustees are willing to involve themselves far more actively in management than they have traditionally done. To provide for increased trustee involvement, the institution should consider the board members' limited time and their need for careful orientation. First, their participation in planning needs to be carefully structured so as not to absorb too large a proportion of the amount of time they have to devote to institutional management. It should be kept in mind that many colleges and universities make heavy, if informal, demands on their trustees for help in raising money, managing investment portfolios, designing buildings, resolving legal problems, and maintaining close relationships with governmental agencies, churches, and other organizations and associations. Recognizing the extent of these other demands on trustees' time, the process outlined in this book limits the trustee role in planning to one of review and approval, which is consistent with their legally mandated responsibility. In addition, however, this new role has the advantage of not requiring them to engage in the time-consuming work of fact-gathering, analysis, and formulation of plans.

The second means of increasing trustee involvement, in planning and also in other areas of management, is to design and implement orientation programs which provide new trustees with a comprehensive picture of the institution's programs, the proper roles of trustees in governance and management, the staff and information resources available to trustees in fulfilling these roles, and the standards that the board as a whole applies in evaluating the performance and contribution of its individual members.

Trustee participation in planning is itself one means of orienting new board members, since the planning process reveals where the institution stands, where it is headed, and what its needs are. Additional orientation is needed, however. One approach is to assign to the board's nominating committee the responsibility for putting on a series of orientation sessions, with each one held just before a full meeting of the board. The entire series might extend over a period of eighteen months to two years, and new trustees could begin the cycle at any time after their appointment.

BUILDING THE EXECUTIVE TEAM

Successful planning usually reflects close collaboration among top managers, since most organizations are too large and too complex to function as the lengthened shadow of any one individual. Critical planning decisions generally cut across organizational boundaries, involving issues of academic programs, governmental and voluntary support, and financial management. These decisions require a high level of coordination among administrators responsible for different areas. The management of most large organizations, therefore, is as heavily dependent on the effectiveness of its group processes as it is on the quality of its technical analysis and decision-making. For this reason, members of the executive group need to have frequent opportunities to examine and improve the way they function as a group.

One means of providing such opportunities is to hold executive retreats at regular intervals throughout the year, preferably on at least a quarterly basis. Away from the pressure of daily business, and in longer meetings and informal discussions, top managers can focus on substantive issues of critical importance while at the same time giving attention to the way they collaborate. Skills need to be developed for such group tasks as identifying all the aspects of a problem, generating ideas for alternative solutions, considering the pros and cons of each alternative from different perspectives, and arriving at solutions that are acceptable to all members of the group.

The planning process itself can be used to develop the skills essential to effective teamwork. Executive retreats can be scheduled to coincide with the four stages of the planning and resource allocation cycle. For example, one retreat could be used to focus on diagnostic questions, a second to discuss mission and goals, a third to review and approve five-year operating plans and annual budgets, and a fourth to evaluate progress and agree on the distribution of rewards to individual managers.

Training Administrators

Administrators of both academic programs and support services will need assistance in carrying out their assigned tasks during the first few planning cycles. Persons who have spent most or all of their professional careers in academic institutions may not be familiar with the techniques of marketing and financial analysis, objective setting, operational planning, and performance evaluation required by the proposed system.

There are several different ways of addressing the need for training and assistance during the early phases of implementation. One approach best suited to small and medium-sized institutions is to let top administrators develop training programs separately for the organizational units under their direction. In support areas, and in the management disciplines of academic units, relatively small amounts of training may suffice. In most undergraduate and graduate programs, however, faculty leaders will need to see concrete examples of how planning tasks are carried out. This assistance could be provided by one or more of the top administrators who would in any case need to be heavily involved in the planning process.

An alternative approach is to form a small staff group in the office of the president or executive vice president. Such a group would provide both training and technical assistance on an institution-wide basis to all managers involved in the planning process and would also be in a position to monitor progress being made in the implementation of the system. This approach, which is best suited to the needs of large institutions, offers the advantages of consistency in training as well as some savings in staff time because of economies of scale.

Timetable for Implementation

The timetable for completing a cycle of the proposed planning system should be tailored to the overall management and governance framework in which the institution is operating, including the requirements of any statewide governing boards, coordinating agencies, and legislative appropriations cycles. This section suggests an approximate timetable that most institutions will need to modify in varying degrees. The following proposed timetable is based on the assumption that the board of trustees or its executive committee meets once each month throughout the year.

The diagnosis of internal trends and external developments and the identification of major planning issues should be completed before the May meeting of the board. A draft of this report first should be circulated among division and support unit heads in April for comments. The final report then should be presented to the board's executive committee. Following its acceptance by the board, the president should distribute the report widely, together with the call for review and possible revisions in statements of mission, goals, and strategies.

The planning stage should be completed prior to the board's October meeting. If necessary, special meetings of the board or its executive committee can be held during this period to consider major changes in program goals or strategies. Upon approval by the board, the planning report should be circulated fully within the institution.

Tasks comprising the resource allocation stage could begin in November with the distribution of guidelines for preparing five-year operating and financial plans. As soon as operating plans have been completed and approved, normally by January, budget guidelines should be announced and the process of developing the annual budget should commence. Even if the institution's total appropriations request must be made much earlier, detailed budgeting should be delayed until plans have been approved and the level of resources available during the coming year can be reliably estimated. Budgets for a fiscal year beginning in July should be developed no earlier than the preceding January, and no later than March, when both enrollment and public appropriations usually can be predicted with sufficient validity.

The last stage in the cycle, evaluation of organizational and individual performance, begins as soon as plans and budgets have been approved and are being implemented. Monthly and quarterly evaluation reports are prepared and reviewed at the same time the next planning cycle is underway and thus overlap with the tasks of diagnosis, setting goals and objectives, and developing plans and budgets.

CONCLUSION

The essential work of planning is deciding on the programs and services the organization should provide, the fundamental policies that should guide the development of these programs, and the competitive role of the organization in its chosen markets. These decisions typify what Marvin Bower has called "the will to manage" in his book of that title (New York, 1966): the desire to control the direction of an organization's growth and development, rather than to let it be swept along by events.

The focus of this book has not been directed at the specific decisions an institution should make, but rather on the process that is used to make those decisions. The strategic planning process is but one of several important processes educational managers need to develop.

Top executives of colleges and universities have a dual role. Their first and most visible role is in managing the organization—identifying problems, making decisions, evaluating results, and appraising individual performance. Their second and equally important responsibility is to build, improve, refine, and formalize the management processes as such—the systems of planning, program evaluation, performance appraisal and fund-raising. Only when these processes are formalized and communicated can they be learned and put to work throughout an organization.

The planning and resource allocation process described in this book is one of six major systems that need to be improved in institutions of higher education. The other processes are:

- Developing an organizational philosophy
- Building the organizational structure
- Recruiting, selecting, and developing personnel
- Raising operating and capital funds
- Activating people

In combination, these systems determine the overall quality of management in an organization. Developing an organizational philosophy clarifies, strengthens, and promotes a set of beliefs and attitudes. In turn, these values give the organization a unique personality and character. In a college or university, an important aspect of this process is deciding which of the traditional practices of an academic community should be preserved and which should be changed. The process of developing an organizational philosophy should also take into account the size of the institution, its location and funding sources, and the characteristics of its principal clientele.

Building the organizational structure includes developing the formal plan of organization that helps people work together cooperatively and constructively: assignments of functional responsibility, reporting relationships, spans of supervisory authority, and flows of work and information.

The process of providing personnel is first and foremost a matter of recruiting and selecting people, including an adequate proportion of highly talented faculty and administrators who can provide leadership and innovation in curriculum development, teaching, and management. A second aspect of this process is identifying staff development needs and designing programs to meet them. One increasingly important dimension of the personnel function is formulating an effective approach to union-management relationships. Building on the academic tradition of collegial governance, colleges and universities need to find ways to achieve a partnership between unions and management that encompasses and transcends the adversary components of collective bargaining.

Raising operating and capital funds is one of the processes that distinguishes higher education management from other managerial styles. Identifying a mix of funding sources, selecting techniques to maintain stable and productive relationships with these sources, and ensuring an adequate flow of capital to meet long-term needs without interruption are the primary aims of this process. In addition, it is to each organization's advantage to develop unique ways of raising funds so as to establish for itself a distinctive image and justification for the support it needs.

A system for activating and energizing individual effort is the sixth and last of the major processes that need to be further developed by educational institutions. The most effective approach has generally been to expand opportunities for self-government by asking managers to become more involved in shaping the policies, plans, and programs they will be asked to carry out. This also limits the need to rely on orders and penalties as negative sources of control. Most administrators are attracted to organizations that provide greater opportunities to advance on the basis of individual merit, to gain a sense of individual achievement, and to have the freedom to act independently within the framework of established policies. Finally, there should be an appropriate mix of rewards — financial and non-financial — to attract and retain capable and highly motivated management talent.

The planning and resource allocation system proposed in this book, together with the five other systems described briefly in this chapter, can help educational managers to design and execute plans for dealing with the internal developments and external forces that influence the long-term effectiveness and social usefulness of the organization as a whole. When formal procedures are in place to focus managers' attention on identifying and assessing the relationship and significance of specific trends and developments, the institution is better equipped to adapt constructively to its environment.

REFERENCES

AGUILAR, F. J. *Scanning the Business Environment.* New York: Macmillan, 1967.

ALLEN, L. A. *Professional Management: New Concepts and Proven Practices.* New York: McGraw-Hill, 1973.

AMERICAN COUNCIL ON EDUCATION. *College and University Business Administration.* Revised edition. Washington, D. C.: American Council on Education, 1968.

ANTHONY, R. N. *Planning and Control Systems: A Framework for Analysis.* Boston: Graduate School of Business Administration, Harvard University, 1965.

ANTHONY, R. N. and HERZLINGER, R. *Management Control in Nonprofit Organizations.* Homewood, Illinois: Richard D. Irwin, Inc., 1975.

BALDERSTON, F. E. *Managing Today's University.* Berkeley: Ford Foundation Program for Research in University Administration, 1974. San Francisco: Jossey-Bass, Inc., 1974.

BARNARD, C. I. *Functions of the Executive.* 30th Anniversary edition. Cambridge, Mass: Harvard University Press, 1968.

BOWEN, H. and DOUGLASS, G. *Efficiency In Liberal Education.* Berkeley: Carnegie Commission on Higher Education, 1973.

BOWEN, W. G., and others. *Budgeting and Resource Allocation at Princeton University.* Princeton, N. J.: Princeton University Press, 1972.

BOWER, M. *The Will to Manage: Corporate Success through Programmed Management.* New York: McGraw-Hill, 1966.

BRADY, R. "MBO Goes To Work in the Public Sector," Harvard Business Review, March-April, 1973.

CARNEGIE COMMISSION ON HIGHER EDUCATION. *More Effective Use of Resources.* New York: McGraw-Hill, 1972.

CASASCO, J. A. *Corporate Planning Models For University Management.* Washington, D. C.: ERIC Clearinghouse on Higher Education, 1970.

CHANDLER, A. D. , JR. *Strategy and Structure: Chapters in the History of the Industrial Enterprise.* Cambridge, Mass.: M.I.T. Press, © 1962.

CHEIT, E. "The Management Systems Challenge." Speech given at the annual meeting of the American Council on Education, Washington, D. C., Fall, 1973.

COMMITTEE FOR ECONOMIC DEVELOPMENT (CED). *Management and Financing of Colleges.* New York, 1973.

DAEDALUS. *American Higher Education: Toward An Uncertain Future.* Volume I, Fall 1974, and Volume II, Winter 1975.

DODDS, H. W. *The Academic President—Educator or Caretaker?* New York: McGraw-Hill, 1962.

DRUCKER, P. F. *Management: Tasks, Responsibilities, Practices.* New York: Harper and Row, 1973.

DRUCKER, P. F. *The Age of Discontinuity: Guidelines to our Changing Society.* New York: Harper and Row, ©1968, 1969.

EWING, D. W. *The Practice of Planning.* New York: Harper and Row, 1968.

FRAM, E. "We Must Market Education," *Chronicle of Higher Education,* April 17, 1972.

HALSTEAD, D. K. *Statewide Planning in Higher Education.* Washington, D. C.: U. S. Office of Education, 1974.

HOFSTEDE, D. H. *The Game of Budget Control.* Assen, The Netherlands: Van Gorcum and Co., N.V., 1967.

HOOS, I. R. *Systems Analysis in Public Policy.* Berkeley: University of California Press, 1972.

INMAN, J. C. *Proposed Procedure for Forward Budget Planning.* Multilithed. Philadelphia: University of Pennsylvania, 1973.

INNER CITY FUND (ICF). *EDANAL: A Computer Model for Preparation and Analysis of Program Budgets.* Washington, D. C.: ICF, 1972.

JEWETT, J. E. *College Admissions Planning.* Berkeley: Ford Foundation Program for Research in University Administration, Report P-23, 1971.

KALUDIS, G., editor. *Strategies for Budgeting.* San Francisco: Jossey-Bass, 1973.

KNOWLES, A. S., editor. *Handbook of College and University Administration.* New York: McGraw-Hill, 1970.

LORANGE, P. and VANCIL, R. F. "How To Design A Strategic Planning System," *Harvard Business Review,* September-October, 1976.

LYDEN, F. J. and MILLER, E. G., editors. *Planning, Programming, Budgeting: A Systems Approach to Management.* Chicago: Markham Publishing, 1968.

MARCH, J. G. and SIMON, H. A. *Organizations.* Graduate School of Industrial Administration, Carnegie Institute of Technology. New York: John Wiley & Sons, Inc., 1958.

MINTZBERG, H. "Planning On The Left Side and Managing On The Right," *Harvard Business Review,* July-August, 1976.

MOYNIHAN, D. P. "The Concept of Public Policy in the 1970s." Speech given at Hendrix College, Conway, Arkansas, April 6, 1970.

NATIONAL CENTER FOR HIGHER EDUCATION MANAGE-MENT SYSTEMS (NCHEMS). *Cost-Finding Principles and Procedures.* Boulder, 1972.

PAREKH, S. B. *Long-Range Planning.* New York: Change Magazine Press, 1977.

PEAT, MARWICK, MITCHELL & CO. *Planning, Budgeting and Accounting.* Washington, D. C.: National Association of College and University Business Officers, 1970.

QUALLS, R. L., DONNELLY, J. H., and BOTTOM, D. C. *Corporate Planning: A Guide for Savings and Loan Associations.* Chicago, Illinois: U.S. League of Savings Associations, 1979.

RUML, B. and MORRISON, D. H. *Memo to a College Trustee: A Report on Financial and Structural Problems of the Liberal College.* New York: McGraw-Hill, 1959.

SHOEMAKER, W. A. *A Systems Approach to College Administration and Planning.* Washington, D. C.: Council for the Advancement of Small Colleges, 1972.

SIMON, H. A. *Administrative Behavior.* New York: Macmillan, 1947.

STEINER, G. A. *Top Management Planning.* New York, Macmillan, 1969.

WAGNER, W. C. and WEATHERSBY, G. B. *Optimality in College Planning.* Berkeley: Ford Foundation Program for Research in University, Report P-22, 1971.

WEATHERSBY, G. B. *Educational Planning and Decision-Making.* Berkeley: Ford Foundation for Research in University Administration, Report P-6, 1970.

WEATHERSBY, G. B., and BALDERSTON, F. E. *PPBS in Higher Education Planning and Management.* Berkeley: Ford Foundation Program for Research in University Administration, Report P-31, 1972.

WILDAVSKY, A. B. *The Politics of the Budgeting Process.* Boston and Toronto: Little, Brown & Co., 1964.

About the Author

John C. Merson is president of the management consulting firm of Merson Associates, Inc. The firm conducts studies of organization, strategic plans, finance, program evaluation, and personnel administration for colleges and universities, for federal and state agencies, and for local school systems. He was educated at Amherst College, the University of North Carolina at Chapel Hill, and the Harvard Business School.

Prior to establishing Merson Associates, Mr. Merson was with Cresap, McCormick, and Paget, Inc. for three years as a management consultant in the firm's Education and Government Services Division. There he planned and directed studies for such institutions and agencies as the University of Pennsylvania, the New School for Social Research, Rhode Island College, the University of Tulsa, the City of New York, and the U.S. Department of Health, Education and Welfare.

Mr. Merson also spent three years, from 1971 to 1974, as a Woodrow Wilson Foundation administrative intern at Lenoir-Rhyne College in North Carolina. During this period he served, consecutively, as Director of Student Financial Aid, Assistant to the President, and Associate Academic Dean.

He has been a member of the Society for College and University Planning, the National Association of College and University Business Officers, the College and University Personnel Association, the American Association for Higher Education, and the American Management Associations.

About the Author

Robert L. Qualls has served as a member of Arkansas Governor Bill Clinton's Cabinet since January 1979. Prior to this appointment, he was President of The College of the Ozarks for five years. Dr. Qualls previously served as a Senior Vice President and Chairman of the Venture Committee of a regional commercial bank and has taught in both private and public colleges and universities. He received his bachelor's and master's degrees from Mississippi State University, and his doctoral work was completed at Louisiana State University. In 1974, he was awarded the Doctor of Laws degree from Whitworth College. Dr. Qualls was formerly a Ford Foundation Faculty Research Fellow at Vanderbilt University and in 1964 he received the Foundation for Economic Education Award.

Dr. Qualls is an active participant in the area of planning, speaking at numerous banking, savings and loan, academic, and governmental meetings across the country, as well as publishing a number of articles on the subject. His most recent publication on this subject was *Corporate Planning: A Guide for Savings and Loan Associations.* This guide was commissioned by the United States League of Savings Associations and was published in 1979. He has also been a consultant to a number of groups in the area of strategic planning.

Dr. Qualls serves as a member of the faculty and thesis advisor at the Stonier Graduate School of Banking at Rutgers University and Marketing Course Coordinator of the Banking School of the South at Louisiana State University. He also serves as lecturer on corporate planning for banks at the Essentials of Banking School at Duke University.